is book will aid in the publications of more educational material from Zini Graphics.

lthough it is a coloring book, it is advised that parents encourge neatness and reading while coloring.

Book and cover designed by Zini Graphics

HOURS OF COLORING

By:

Nadja Morgan

&

David Walters

ZG

ZG

Lets Drive

I AM ON TOP OF THE WORLD!

I am an adult Elephant

I am backpack and he is Map

DRAW YOUR FAVORITE PICTURES

LOOKING NICE

Lets fly around the world

I am Cow, you can get milk from me

Wait! I want to fly too!

HEY ! I AM A CRAB

Pretty Huh?

I AM A GERIFFE, I AM TALL

DRAW YOUR FAVORITE PICTURES

Hop Hop and Away

Can I Come too

What A Plane

1-Brown 2-Red 3-Green 4-Yellow

FOUR COLORS SHOW WHO I AM

I AM A DINOSAUR, I EAT LEAVES

TODAY IS MY BIRTHDAY

DRAW YOUR FAVORITE PICTURES

I NEED A LITTLE COLOR IN LIFE

I AM MAMA DINOSAUR

Can I come to the party

Its Sponge Bob Square pant

Let the party begin

Everything is just beautiful

Hey I am Sandy

DRAW YOUR FAVORITE PICTURES

Plant me in your garden

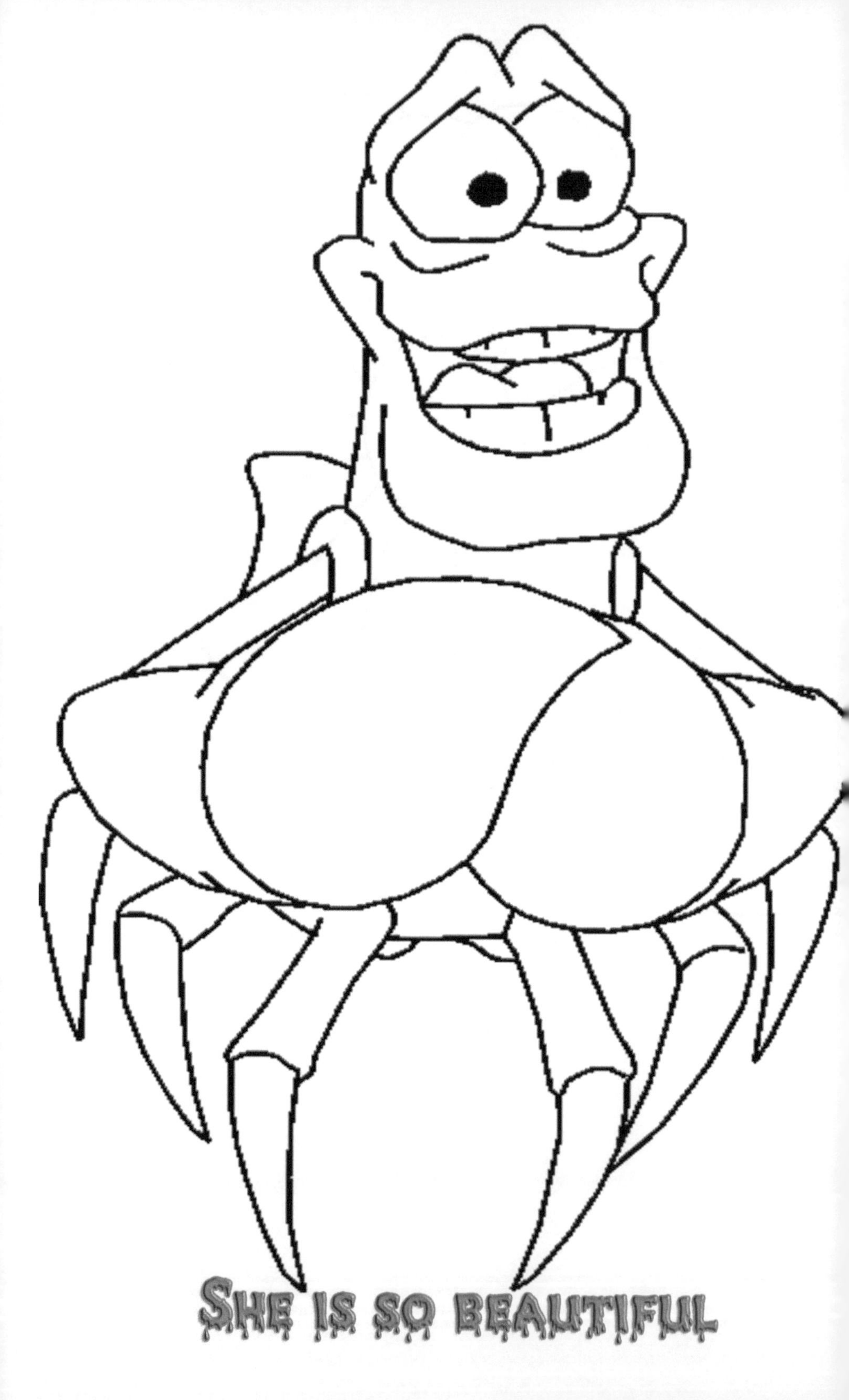
She is so beautiful

Lets Dance

DRAW YOUR FAVORITE PICTURES

Connect the dots from 1

So Cute!

99, 100 HERE I COME

I AM SO LUCKY

Can you jump as high as me?

HEY WHATS HAPPENING HERE?

There is cake in the kitchen

Having fun

Spin Ball Spin

I'LL SING A SONG, YOU SING ALONG

DRAW YOUR FAVORITE PICTURES

This is my family

Lets go for a swim

That looks like fun

Come join the fun

Hey come hop around with tigga

ETS SING A SONG

What a party, loving it!

I WISH IT WAS MY PARTY

Yeh come dance with me

Please color me

Good Night The Party Is ove

DRAW YOUR FAVORITE PICTURES

LETS GO HOME

What A Day

Done Already?

HOURS OF COLORING

CONTACT US

BWERECORDS@YAHOO.CO.UK

1-876-414-6376

ZINI.BWERECORDS@YAHOO.CO.UK

1-876-895-2841